Exploring Indian Mythology

Don Nardo

San Diego, CA

About the Author

Classical historian and award-winning author Don Nardo has written numerous acclaimed volumes about ancient civilizations and peoples. They include more than three dozen overviews of the mythologies of the Sumerians, Babylonians, Egyptians, Greeks, Romans, Persians, Celts, Chinese, Aztecs, Native Americans, and others. Nardo, who also composes and arranges orchestral music, lives with his wife, Christine, in Massachusetts.

© 2023 ReferencePoint Press, Inc.
Printed in the United States

For more information, contact:
ReferencePoint Press, Inc.
PO Box 27779
San Diego, CA 92198
www.ReferencePointPress.com

ALL RIGHTS RESERVED.
No part of this work covered by the copyright hereon may be reproduced or used in any form or by any means—graphic, electronic, or mechanical, including photocopying, recording, taping, web distribution, or information storage retrieval systems—without the written permission of the publisher.

Picture Credits:

6: Vectomart/Shutterstock
9: AstroVed.com/Shutterstock
10: Dinodia Photos/Alamy Stock Photo
15: The Stapleton Collection/Bridgeman Images
19: Patel251280/Shutterstock
21: © Look and Learn/Bridgeman Images
25: Archivart/Alamy Stock Photo
29: Well/BOT/Alamy Stock Photo
31: Art Collection/Alamy Stock Photo
35: Sabena Jane Blackbird/Alamy Stock Images
39: Storm Is Me/Shutterstock
40: Tosporn Preede/Alamy Stock Image
44: Godong/Alamy Stock Image
48: Guru Ji Creation/Shutterstock
50: mifotodigital.club/Shutterstock
54: The Picture Art Collection/Alamy Stock Image

LIBRARY OF CONGRESS CATALOGING-IN-PUBLICATION DATA

Names: Nardo, Don, 1947- author.
Title: Exploring Indian mythology / Don Nardo.
Description: San Diego, CA : ReferencePoint Press, Inc., 2023. | Includes
   bibliographical references and index.
Identifiers: LCCN 2022021943 (print) | LCCN 2022021944 (ebook) | ISBN
   9781678204808 (library binding) | ISBN 9781678204815 (ebook)
Subjects: LCSH: Hindu mythology--Juvenile literature. | Mythology,
   Indic--Juvenile literature.
Classification: LCC BL1216 .N369 2023 (print) | LCC BL1216 (ebook) | DDC
   294.5/13--dc23/eng/20220607
LC record available at https://lccn.loc.gov/2022021943
LC ebook record available at https://lccn.loc.gov/2022021944

Contents

Introduction   4
Universal, Epic Themes

Chapter One   8
The Creation of the Universe

Chapter Two   18
Good Versus Evil

Chapter Three   28
War and Warriors

Chapter Four   38
Karma and Destiny

Chapter Five   47
Fabled Animals

Source Notes   57
Key Hindu Gods   59
For Further Research   60
Index   62

INTRODUCTION

Universal, Epic Themes

Long ago, in an era that time has largely forgotten, Yama, the Hindu god of death—a humorless, no-nonsense, scary figure—had a moment of weakness. In a temporary expression of decency and kindness, he married a mortal woman with whom he had a son named Yama Kumar. Unlike the father, whose main preoccupation was overseeing the transition of human souls from life to the afterlife, the boy came to devote himself to the art of healing. The outgoing, caring Yama Kumar grew up to become a doctor and renowned authority on medicinal herbs.

There came a day when the younger Yama, then in his twenties, faced a situation that clearly demonstrated his gentle and generous nature. News came that a princess in a nearby kingdom had been stricken with a mysterious illness that her father's physicians were powerless to combat. Hoping that his own wide knowledge of medicine would be helpful, Yama Kumar hastily traveled to that neighboring nation and offered his services. Sincerely thankful for that gesture, the local king welcomed him.

The visitor was filled with optimism, until he entered the princess's bedchamber. There, to his surprise and dismay, he saw his own father standing at the foot of her sickbed. Clearly, the lord of death was getting ready to transport the young woman to the depths of the underworld. Yama Kumar approached the grim-looking deity and beseeched him to leave and allow the princess to live. Yama paused and considered this plea, and after a few moments, out of love for his son, he proposed a temporary deal. The god offered to allow the young woman to cling to life for three more days. After that, if no cure was found, he would return and take her to the realm of the dead.

No sooner had Yama vanished from the room than his son initiated a round-the-clock flurry of attempts to cure the ailing princess. The young physician tried every treatment then known to humanity and even concocted several new and experimental herbal combinations. Unfortunately for his patient, however, none of these endeavors were successful, and she remained gravely ill.

When the last minutes of the third day came, as expected, the death deity arrived, ready to claim the princess's soul. But in a last-ditch effort, Yama Kumar resorted to trickery. He convinced his father that a fellow god, whom the deity of death hated, was about to enter the room. Believing this, and eager to avoid contact with that rival divinity, Yama hurriedly slipped away. His absence gave his son time to find a cure, and the princess recovered. Subsequently, she and Yama Kumar fell in love and married, bringing the two kingdoms closer than they had ever been.

Filled with Magical Elements

Stories like that of Yama Kumar—about love and lovers—abound in Hindu mythology. Yet love is only one of many powerful, often epic themes expressed in the thousands of surviving myths from ancient India. Among these universal ideas, concepts, and topics are the creation of the universe and humanity, religious devotion, good versus evil, the recurring horrors of war, and human destiny. The people of ancient India consistently developed these and other similar themes in highly colorful ways. The enduring myths are typically crammed with descriptions of picturesque landscapes; magnificent castles and palaces; sweeping, bloody battles; frequent divine interventions; and plenty of living beings with magical powers.

divine intervention
The direct involvement of a god or gods in human affairs

Regarding the latter, writes historian George M. Williams, Hindu mythology "utilizes magic so freely that one cannot easily gain attention without it. Thus, India's mythology seems filled to a higher degree with magical or miraculous elements than [most] other mythologies are." He adds that "the supernatural adorns almost everything"[1] in these ancient tales.

Stories Still Told and Retold

Another crucial element makes the Indian myths particularly memorable, as well as markedly different from the stories in most other world mythologies. Namely, the traditional Hindu stories make up a *living*, rather than a *dead*, mythology. Williams explains, "A living mythology is quite different from a dead one. One does not study Hindu mythology in the same way one studies Greek mythology. . . . There are still hundreds of millions of Hindus who appropriate [fit] Hindu mythology into their own lives in a variety of ways."[2]

Indeed, most of India's residents today still tell and retell the old myths and revel in the memorable fantastical characters contained in them. University professors Roy Amore and Larry Shinn point out, "To grow up in India is to mature in a world alive with demons and water nymphs, goblins, and irate goddesses. Wisdom is often measured not by [college] degrees or formal education, but by the ability to tell the right story. . . . Mothers and fathers teach their children religious and family responsibilities through stories."[3]

Noted Indian actress and storyteller Madhur Jaffrey remembers her own parents telling those age-old tales. They had been repeated in her family, she says, "generation after generation for centuries." Those stories "were designed not only to separate right from wrong, but to prepare us [for] the vagaries of life and the fact of death."[4] After everyone now alive has passed away, she adds, the Indian myths will continue to be told, "to remind us that we do not know everything [and] to teach us that our values are constant."[5]

CHAPTER ONE

The Creation of the Universe

At first there was nothing but a monstrously huge, dark sea that seemed to stretch away forever in all directions. Brahman, the single, all-powerful deity composed of spirit rather than flesh, floated leisurely just above the water's surface. He drifted there, always deep in thought, for a thousand years (or what to him was a mere instant) until the idea of creating a universe to surround the sea came to him. He had fashioned that great expanse of water by willing it into existence long before. But by itself, he felt, it had seemed incomplete.

To create an entire universe, Brahman realized, would take some hard work. And for that, he felt he would do better in corporeal, or flesh-and-blood, form. To that end, he willed a special seed into existence and watched it sink silently beneath the waves. Seconds later, he no longer floated above the vast sea. Instead, he now resided within the submerged seed, which steadily transformed into a magnificent glowing egg. In time (how long no one knows), the egg rose to the surface and split open, revealing a large, luxurious lotus blossom.

Lying within the flower's folds, fast asleep, was the creator god Brahma. According to later Hindu myth tellers, this avatar, or manifestation, of the universal spirit Brahman had four

> **corporeal**
> Composed of flesh and blood, or having a body

Brahma, the four-headed god of creation, produces a seed that blossoms into a luxurious lotus flower to help him bring the universe to life.

heads. And from time to time each of them recited one of the four Vedas, the oldest of Hinduism's sacred texts. Brahma also had red skin and four arms. One of his hands held a book of prayers from the Vedas; a second hand held a spoon or flower; a third a pot of water; and the fourth a string of prayer beads. In addition, he moved along the surface of the giant lotus's leaves atop a handsome white swan, his *vahana*. Each of the Hindu gods who would subsequently be created was destined to ride on his or her own such animal.

Fashioning the Four Worlds

The creator deity felt as if he had awakened from a long sleep. He yawned, rubbed his eyes, stretched, and glanced around at his surroundings. At first it appeared as though he was alone, hovering there above the surface of the seemingly limitless sea. But soon he caught sight of an unidentified object floating toward him on the water's surface.

Finally, the object came close enough for Brahma to see that it was a huge serpent whose body was twisted into several coils nested within one another. Moreover, huddled inside those coils was the divinity Vishnu. Another incarnation of the universal spirit, he bore a muscular body that shone with a radiant blue hue. He, too, possessed four arms, and his hands held, in succession, a

Atop the splendid eagle Garuda, Vishnu holds a mace, a lotus flower, a conch shell, and a discus in his four hands.

mace (club), a lotus flower, a conch shell, and a discus. Although sleeping, the blue being was mounted atop his vahana, the splendid eagle Garuda.

> **vahana**
> In ancient Indian lore, a creature ridden by a god

Assuming that Vishnu needed his rest, Brahma politely refrained from waking him. But suddenly came a loud noise—a mysterious humming sound that echoed across the sea's surface. It became so intense that it awakened the sleeping god. As he opened his eyes, a bright flash of light illuminated the dark ocean and sky. Brahma looked outward and saw that a brilliant glowing disk—the sun—now hung on the distant horizon. Clearly, the first dawn of a new age had arrived.

Vishnu's instantaneous formation of the sun to light the new world is a reminder that Hindu mythology contains numerous alternate creation stories. In some of these stories, Vishnu, rather than Brahma, is the primary creator. In one of those myths, the blue deity initially took the form of a giant boar. Reaching into his navel, he extracted a lotus blossom from which Brahma soon emerged. Then, with Brahma's help, Vishnu went into a veritable frenzy of creation. According to an early Hindu holy text, the *Vishnu Purana*:

> He lifted the earth up quickly and placed [it] upon the great ocean. The earth stayed like a great ship on the top of the flood of water and did not sink, because [its] body was so spread out. Then, when he had made the earth level, the [creator] . . . piled up mountains on the earth in order to divide it. By means of his power, [that great god] divided the earth into seven continents [and] he created the four worlds [earth, the atmosphere, the heavens, and the underworld].[6]

In the popular version in which Vishnu assists Brahma, the two gods fashioned the four worlds from the separate petals of Brahma's birth lotus. One petal expanded outward and became earth's surface, a second petal rose up to form the atmosphere, the third one sank downward and became the underworld, and the fourth floated up beyond the atmosphere and morphed into the night sky containing the luminous stars and planets.

New Deities, Animals, and Plants Arise

Fashioning the physical structure of the universe and earth marked only the beginning of Brahma's and Vishnu's creative endeavors. Overflowing with inventive and artistic energy, they next set out to populate the world with other living things. Perhaps partly because they were incarnations of the sole god, Brahman, they decided to continue that process of making avatars. In that mindset they started making new versions of themselves, and in turn many of the divine beings they spawned created *their* own avatars.

> **avatar**
> A manifestation, incarnation, or alternate form of a living thing

In this manner, numerous new gods and goddesses arose. Among them were Agni, god of fire; Devi, god of light; Ganesha, god of wisdom; and Vayu, god of wind, whose own avatar, in some Indian traditions, was the monkey-headed Hanuman, god of strength and courage. Similarly, Lakshmi, goddess of wealth, subsequently gave rise to her own avatar—Radha, goddess of love.

Meanwhile, even as some of the gods were begetting still more deities, Brahma and Vishnu proceeded to fashion all sorts of animals. According to the *Vishnu Purana*, for instance, Brahma "made the birds from his own youthful energy; he made sheep from his breast, goats from his mouth; [he] created cows from his stomach and his two sides. From his feet he made horses, elephants, donkeys, oxen, deer, camels, mules, antelopes, and other species. Grasses, fruits, and roots were born from the hairs of his body."[7]

To help with making still more diverse beings and creatures, Brahma transformed his thumbs into a special assistant creator named Daksha. Depicted in later Indian art as a pot-bellied individual with a goat's head, Daksha was said to have the power to make himself extremely small. In this state he created life

The Creator's Many Forms

The story of how Brahma and Vishnu, with the aid of Daksha, created the universe and the living things within it does more than tell where the world, animals, plants, and humans came from. The tale also illustrates the role of Brahman. Because he is often mentioned along with Brahma, Vishnu, Daksha, and other gods, at first glance it might seem as though Hinduism is polytheistic, meaning that its adherents worship multiple deities. Beneath the surface, however, Hinduism is actually monotheistic, like Judaism, Christianity, and Islam. Hindus refer to the sole god who created and controls the universe not only as Brahman, but also as the *ishvara*, or "universal spirit." Thus, all of the many divine beings in the Hindu pantheon (group of gods) are not truly separate entities. Rather, they are diverse manifestations or disguises that the ishvara employs in his roles of creator, guide, controller, and protector of the world and humanity. Hindus believe that all matter in the universe—both living and nonliving—is an expression of one kind or another of the ishvara.

forms that sprang from tiny seeds and eggs. He also gave rise to snakes and various wild animals, along with ghosts, demons, and the Gandharvas—celestial beings who were adept at singing and dancing.

Brahma, Vishnu, and Daksha were so busy with this immense round of making nonliving and living things that they gave little or no thought to the fact that these efforts were not unique. Whether they produced divine avatars, camels and elephants, or serpents and ghosts, theirs was not the first such burst of creation. Nor would it be the last. Rather, the universe they made was merely the latest version of universal creation—a single link in an endless chain of new universes.

This is because Hindus believe that time has no beginning, nor will it have an end. Instead, time, the rise of divine beings, and their creation of the natural world are seen as cyclic and eternal. That is, in each new cycle, the gods and world come into existence, flourish for a while, and then decline and die out, thereby making way for the next cycle of creation. The length of each cycle is unknown. The general wisdom is that a single cycle lasts a few billion years. Therefore, the *Vishnu Purana* states, at the start of each cycle, "again and again Brahma performs creation of this sort, for his power is the will to create."[8]

The Creation of Humans

Driven by that powerful determination to create, Brahma was not satisfied with bringing into existence the sky, mountains, plains, forests, animals, and plants. There was something missing, he felt. But what could it be? After pondering that problem for several minutes, he suddenly realized that what the new universe lacked was a race of intelligent mortal beings to populate that vast, diverse world. The creator deity also reasoned that such beings could potentially serve as loyal followers and worshippers of Brahman's numerous divine manifestations.

The race of beings in question became known as humans. Brahma fashioned the first one and called him Manu. Hinduism has several different traditions that describe Manu, his adventures, and his hand in the creation of the rest of humanity. Almost certainly the most famous and popular version is the one in which one day that initial human went for a walk along the bank of the Indus River. He was surprised to hear a faint voice crying out for help. Glancing around, he spied a tiny fish flopping around in the mud, and it became clear that the creature could speak. According to the ancient Indian document the *Satapatha Brahmana*, the fish told Manu, "Care for me and I will save you."[9] When the man asked what he needed to be saved from, the creature explained that a huge flood was soon going to inundate the earth's surface and that the fish could keep Manu from drowning in the disaster.

Manu believed the fish's story and carefully cared for the creature. At first he placed it in a bucket of fresh water. Later, as the

The blue-skinned god Vishnu, disguised as a fish, warned the first human, Manu, of a great flood that would soon cover the earth. As instructed, Manu built a boat to save himself and other living creatures.

fish grew bigger, Manu dug a trench and filled it with clean water. The fish thrived. It became much larger and grew a massive horn on top of its head.

Then the creature revealed more to the man about the coming flood. Manu needed to build a large boat, the fish stated. In another ancient text, the creature continued, "In a short time the earth will be submerged in water." The creatures "born of sweat, those born of eggs, or of water . . . place them all into this boat and save them, for they have no protector. And when your ship is struck by the [powerful] winds . . . fasten the ship to this horn of mine."[10]

The Hindu Creation and Modern Dance

Since ancient times Hindus have expressed reverence for their gods through the arts, often in the medium of dance. Several traditional Indian dances developed to honor and imitate one form of the major god Shiva: Nataraja, also known as the Lord of the Dance. In some Indian traditions, the vibrations from his "cosmic" dance steps helped create the universe. "The cosmic dance is the dance of life itself, including creation," says Swami Venkataraman, a spokesperson for the Hindu American Foundation, which represents the more than 3 million American Hindus. "Dance is the only art that cannot stand by itself without the artist. One can observe and enjoy paintings, sculptures, [and] poetry . . . but there is no dance without the dancer being present and visible in the moment. It is a powerful way of showing God is [inherent] in all of creation. The creator and creation are inseparable."

Swami Venkataraman, "The Symbolism of Nataraja, the Cosmic Dancer," Hindu American Foundation, February 16, 2022. www.hinduamerican.org.

Sure enough, the deluge came, and the great winds, too. Manu had done as the fish had told him by placing all sorts of living things in the boat. He had also run a rope from the ship's bow to the fish's horn. That creature swam forward at the water's surface, pulling the ship along with it and thereby keeping it from sinking. After a few weeks, when the floodwaters subsided, the man stepped off the boat onto the dry land. It was then that the fish appeared again and, to Manu's astonishment, swiftly transformed itself into a magnificent blue-skinned being. He had never been truly a fish at all, the being explained, but rather was the god Vishnu in disguise.

Soon after that, the creator deity Brahma paid Manu a visit. Walking beside the god was a young woman whose name, Brahma said, was Shatarupa. Brahma had recently created her so that Manu could have a wife and companion. In the years that followed, these first two humans had many children, who themselves had their own offspring, and in this way the human race expanded and spread across earth's surface.

Great Reverence for the Almighty Spirit

With the ascendancy of humans, Brahma and the other divinities who had been aiding him at last felt that their work was done. Creation was complete (at least for this particular universe among countless ones to come). In time, many of the humans adopted the Hindu faith, which views the sole, almighty spirit Brahman with great reverence. After all, Hindus believe it was he who, through his divine avatars, fashioned all that exists. Among the many hymns of thanks that Hinduism developed to honor that majestic deity is one that says, "You have always existed, just as dust, that sits in the air. Who can capture you, who can kill you, whose arrows can make you subservient, who else exists that's so inexplicable and mysterious? You cannot die, you are immortal, [and] for you, day and night have no meaning. . . . O' chief of the highest heaven, help make known to us, that which is yet unknown."[11]

CHAPTER TWO

Good Versus Evil

The drooling, lice-ridden, repulsive Keshi crept through some underbrush lining a large, fertile meadow. Resembling a large, horribly deformed horse with several rows of razor-sharp teeth, the dim-witted demon eyed his intended prey. The latter, a young man named Krishna, was playing a ball game with some farm maidens in the middle of the field.

Not long before, a wicked king named Kamsa had hired the equally evil Keshi to locate and kill Krishna, who that ruler worried might eventually overthrow him. It had taken the demon several months to find the young man. Now, finally, the time had come to slay and devour the object of the search.

What Keshi did not realize was that the person he was about to attack was no ordinary human. Rather, the young man in the field was an avatar of one of the most powerful of all the gods—Vishnu. According to some surviving ancient Indian texts, Krishna had blue skin, like his true self, Vishnu, and was strikingly handsome and multitalented. According to the popular modern Indian thinker and writer Sadhguru, Krishna was an expert dancer and lover, as well as an effective politician and statesman. Moreover, Sadhguru writes, "different people saw different facets of who [Krishna] was." For some, he was primarily a wondrous and personable divine being, while for others he was best known as a skilled and fierce warrior, "a ruthless vanquisher of his foes."[12]

It was Krishna's formidable fighting abilities that Keshi was about to witness firsthand. Blissfully unaware of the danger he was in, the horse demon suddenly sprang forward and galloped as fast as he could toward his target. Krishna saw Keshi approaching but stood his ground. Unafraid, he smiled and at the last moment calmly but swiftly evaded the attacker, who tripped and went sailing face-first onto the ground.

The astonished and enraged monster managed to pull himself back up to his feet and rushed at Krishna once more. This time the demon opened his mouth wide, apparently intending to swallow his prey whole. Still reacting in a calm, unperturbed manner, the blue-skinned youth abruptly jammed an arm into Keshi's mouth. Less than a second later, the arm expanded in size, initially choking the attacker and then causing his head to explode. The

Krishna, one of Vishnu's many avatars, is described as having blue skin and strikingly good looks. Additionally, Krishna is famous for his skills as a ferocious warrior.

demon's lifeless torso then collapsed into the grass, and reacting as though nothing at all had happened, Krishna serenely turned and walked away.

A Wide Variety of Evil Beings

The brief but gory fight between Krishna and Keshi is a classic version of a theme explored often in world mythologies, including that of ancient India—the age-old contest between good and evil. Indeed, the Hindu myths feature a good many villains that cause all manner of troubles for human society.

A lot of those malign characters were demons, of which there were several kinds. One of the scarier ones consisted of the serpent demons, the Nagas. "Their bodies are human to the waist," says noted modern myth teller Veronica Ions, "but end in serpents' tails."[13] The Nagas most often lived in rivers, where they sometimes posed a threat to people riding in boats or walking along riverbanks.

Another variety of evil being consisted of the Pishachas, or flesh-eating demons, who had big red eyes filled with unsightly swollen veins. Fond of caves and other dark places, these monsters were thought to have certain magical abilities that made them very dangerous. They could shape-shift into human or animal form, for example, as well as become invisible and suck energy out of human bodies.

Perhaps the most fearsome and malicious category of demon was that of the Rakshasas. Very hairy, even gorilla-like in many ways, they sometimes formed demon armies that launched large-scale attacks on human towns. The Rakshasas were adept at disguising themselves. Female Rakshasas, for instance, frequently assumed the form of beautiful women. That way they could render human men defenseless by bewitching them. In their natural, undisguised form, Ions writes, the Rakshasas took numerous different physi-

Rakshasas
Hairy, gorilla-like demons that are the archenemies of humans

The fearsome and malicious demons known as Rakshasas took various physical forms. Some resembled dwarfs while others had large bellies; tall, skinny bodies; or animal heads.

cal forms. "Some are dwarfs," she says, while others look "like beanstalks; some [are] fat, others emaciated; some have overlong arms; some only one eye, or only one ear; some have monstrous bellies; some have crooked legs, some one leg, some three and four; some have serpents' heads, other have donkeys', horses', or elephants' heads."[14]

The Rakshasas also broke down into separate groups defined by their habits. The Panis, for instance, were able to fly, which allowed them to sweep down onto unsuspecting travelers. The Grahas hung around battlefields and tried to make soldiers go insane. The Darbas lurked in cemeteries, looking for fresh human corpses to devour.

Darbas
Demons that lurk in cemeteries and devour human corpses

Human Versus Divine Heroes

The ancient Indian myths are filled with other malicious characters, some of them supernatural beings and others humans. The supernatural ones are defined variously as evil spirits, demons, or

Bhima Versus Baka

The great ancient Indian epic the *Mahabharata* includes many myths involving good versus evil. Some feature humans fighting humans. Others depict humans battling monsters. Among the latter is the exciting confrontation between the hero Bhima and the detestable demon Baka. A member of a major Indian family, the Pandavas, Bhima was highly skilled in the use of many weapons, as well as strong and fearless. One day he received word that a demon named Baka had invaded the territory overseen by the Pandavas. Eyewitnesses reported that the hideous beast was taller than a two-story house and devoured people almost whole. Wasting no time, Bhima leaped into action. To achieve the element of surprise, he disguised himself as a simple farmer and purposely walked along the country road located near the cave where Baka ate his victims. Sure enough, the demon fell for the ruse. Thinking Bhima to be largely defenseless, the creature rushed out of the cave and charged right at Bhima. At the last moment, the hero threw off his disguise, wrestled his opponent to the ground, and snapped his spine, which killed the demon instantly.

monsters, depending on the story and the traditions of the region where a specific tale originated. Among these evil beings are the Pretas, spirits of malformed fetuses that died in their mothers' wombs, and the Bhoots, ghosts of humans who died violently and did not have a proper funeral. The human villains, meanwhile, include evil kings and other rulers, along with their henchmen.

Likewise, some of the characters who opposed the villains in the Indian myths are human. They represent the finest aspects of humanity—qualities such as strength, courage, honesty, wisdom, and loyalty. Of their number, one of the most famous and beloved is Arjuna, the principal hero of the great ancient epic the *Mahabharata*. A complex, exciting, *Game of Thrones*–like story, it tells in part how Arjuna overcame a villainous ruler named Jayadratha.

Arjuna's son, Abhimanyu, became another beloved human hero, as did Bhima, who killed several monstrous demons.

No less important among the forces of goodness in the Hindu myths are several divine heroes. Vishnu's avatar Krishna, who slew the horse demon Keshi, is prominent among them. And another avatar of the blue-skinned deity—Rama—was arguably the greatest heroic figure in all of ancient Indian mythology. The primary character in the other pivotal ancient Indian epic—the *Ramayana*—he fought and killed Ravana, the bestial, supremely evil king of Lanka, an entire kingdom populated by demons.

The Battle in the Clouds

Well before Lanka's and Ravana's rise, however, as well as prior to the widespread worship of Vishnu and his avatars, India's chief divine demon slayer was Indra. During the country's Vedic age (around 1500 BCE–500 CE), when the Hindu faith was in its formative stages, Indra was both the war deity and chief god. And he set an early example of how to fight and slay demons.

In that dimly remembered era, a majority of India's inhabitants were farmers who relied on periodic rains for the water they needed to grow their crops. Unfortunately for them, the time came when they no longer had sufficient water for irrigation. This was because the powerful and frightening demon Vritra, who dwelled in the clouds, was siphoning off most of the atmospheric moisture for himself.

Among the many deities to whom the farmers prayed for help were the earth goddess Prithivi and the sky god Dyaus. Neither of those gods was willing to tackle Vritra, however, because he was considerably more physically powerful than they were. Nevertheless, fate had ordained that the dilemma both the farmers and deities found themselves in was not as hopeless as it appeared. Prithivi found that she was pregnant; she soon gave birth to a new divinity. She named him Indra.

From the start, the young god showed every indication that he was special. As a child he was amazingly energetic and strong and rapidly learned to fight with every known weapon, as well as to drive a chariot at dizzyingly high speeds. Moreover, young Indra made it clear that he was not the least bit scared of the cloud demon, Vritra, and was determined to destroy him. Seizing a large thunderbolt, he jumped onto a chariot and rode off into the sky to confront the enemy.

As the chariot bearing the young god sped along, many of the farmers caught sight of it, and they raised their voices in a hymn to their new champion. They called him the lord of thunder and wished him well with all their hearts. Indra heard them, and their confidence in him made him feel even more certain that he could defeat Vritra.

Minutes later, the daring charioteer arrived at the cloud the demon was then inhabiting and raced into it. Vritra immediately heard the clamor of the flying horses that pulled the vehicle and demanded to know who the intruder was. Indra boldly identified himself as Prithivi's son, and the demon reacted with laughter. Surely, Vritra shouted, the pathetic upstart who had dared to invade his privacy must have a death wish. To that, Indra replied that indeed he did have a death wish; only it was Vritra's death that he sought!

These audacious words sent the demon into a colossal rage, and he rushed at Indra, confident that someone a mere one-tenth his size would be quite easy to defeat. This assumption, it turned out, was sorely mistaken. Though far smaller than his opponent, Indra was a good deal stronger and more resolute. According to the account of the battle in the *Mahabharata*, the young god "maimed Vritra by chopping off his right arm." Thoroughly shocked and suddenly fearful, the demon tried hurling an iron club with his left hand, but Indra proceeded to "cut off his other arm also." Then, as Vritra bellowed and staggered around in a daze, Indra decided to deliver the death blow. The intrepid young deity "ripped Vritra's belly open" and barely a second later hurled his thunderbolt, which struck the demon squarely in the chest. "The mighty Vritra lay dead,"[15] the *Mahabharata* states.

The Power of the Female Spirit

Another divine adversary of evil who acquired a potent reputation as a demon slayer was Durga, the Hindu goddess of justice and compassion. Her principal demonic opponent was Mahishasura, who came to be called the Buffalo Demon because of the large horns that grew from the sides of his head. When Mahishasura was young, the story goes, he asked his father why the gods were so often victorious over the demons in battle. The father answered that one reason for it was that the heavenly beings were extremely strong.

In the years that followed, Mahishasura remembered what his father had said. The Buffalo Demon was determined to become stronger than any of the gods so that he could eventually defeat them and seize control of the universe. Day after day, year after

The powerful goddess Durga defeats the Buffalo Demon with a spear to the heart. This intense fight continued for over an hour.

year, Mahishasura religiously employed exercise, diet, meditation, and other means to make himself stronger. And these efforts paid off. In time he became so strong that he felt confident in challenging the gods. Moreover, he soundly defeated several of them and forced the others to retreat.

In the words of the late, popular Indian poet Deepa Agarwal, one of those humiliated deities complained that no one was "strong enough to destroy this evil creature. Let us use our combined powers to create one." Up to that time, all the defeated deities had been male, so it was agreed that the new one should be female instead. "The desperate gods closed their eyes," Agarwal wrote,

From Myth to Modern Movie

One of the major cultural legacies of the ancient Hindu myths is that several of them have been transformed into popular films. One of the most creative of these projects is the 2001 production *Lagaan: Once Upon a Time in India*, directed by noted Indian filmmaker Ashutosh Gowariker. In the story, a British officer, Captain Russell, administers an Indian province during the 1890s, when Britain still ruled India. A terrible drought is ongoing, and Russell makes things worse by levying a crippling tax on the locals. A young peasant boy, Bhuvan, challenges Russell to a cricket match. A deal is struck stipulating that if Bhuvan wins the match, Russell must remove the tax. In the film's finale, Bhuvan's team wins the contest, and the local Indians rejoice. According to Vilnius University scholar Deimantas Valanciunas, "The structural composition of *Lagaan*'s narrative resembles [that] of the famous [Hindu] myth about the thunder god Indra and his battle with [the demon] Vritra. . . . Following the myth, we can replace the demon Vritra with Captain Russell . . . while Bhuvan corresponds to Indra, or the cultural hero. The cricket match then could be interpreted as the cosmogonic battle in the myth."

Deimantas Valanciunas, "Myth in Constructing Contemporary Indian Identity in Popular Hindi Film: The Case of Ashutosh Gowariker," *Acta Orientalia Vilnensia*, 2008. www.journals.vu.lt.

"and began to concentrate all their thoughts on creating this invincible woman. Their divine powers and deep concentration worked, and soon a fiery pillar of light appeared in the sky. It was so bright that even the gods found it impossible to look at it. It was a mass of pure energy produced from their combined power."[16]

When Mahishasura heard that a new goddess—named Durga—had been created to oppose him, he laughed and dismissed the idea that he could be beaten by a mere woman. He was by this time certain that he was invincible. And he decided to seek out Durga and make an example of her. The battle between the two took place on an open plain, and the forces of good and evil lined up on opposite sides of the expanse to watch. The furious fight lasted for over an hour, and contrary to his expectations, the Buffalo Demon got the worst of it. In the end, Durga pinned him down and drove a spear through his heart.

A number of modern mythologists and other scholars believe that humanity can learn something from this myth. Perhaps, says Laura Amazzone, author of a book about the power of the female spirit in history, supernatural females like Durga might help humanity utilize the powers of love and goodness. Durga, she says, "may not solve all the world's problems at the moment, but as this ancient scripture teaches, she is the impenetrable place of calm within our hearts from which we can choose actions that promote harmony and unity rather than selfish harmful acts. . . . We need only invoke Durga to help us remember our true nature and that divine love conquers all."[17]

CHAPTER THREE

War and Warriors

Long ago, somewhere in north-central India, a new demon—one the gods had not encountered before—suddenly appeared on the scene. In and of itself, this was not unusual. Unfamiliar demons did arise from time to time. When that happened either a god or human hero stepped forward to fight and destroy the intruder.

This demon, whose name was Taraka, was different from others, however. He arrived with an army of thousands of demons and openly declared war on the gods and the human race. Indeed, Taraka announced that he intended to destroy all the gods and either kill or enslave the humans.

In the face of this oncoming danger, the gods turned to their young war leader, Kartikeya, who amassed an army of his own, consisting of both deities and humans. As the two armies marched toward each other, Taraka bragged to his followers that he was both a brilliant military general and the strongest demon who had ever existed. So his army would surely win. On the other side, meanwhile, Kartikeya bolstered the confidence of his own soldiers. They had the power of divine goodness backing them, he said. Therefore, they could be confident of victory.

Less than a day later, the opposing armies clashed, and blood was spilled on an immense scale. The great fifth-century-CE Indian epic poet Kalidasa described it, writing in part:

Blood-dripping swords reflected bright
The sunbeams in that awful fight;
Fire-darting like the lightning-flash,
They showed how mighty heroes clash. . . .

The swords that sheaths no longer clasped,
That hands of heroes firmly grasped,
Flashed out in glory through the fight,
As if they laughed in mad delight.[18]

As the battle raged on, Kartikeya guided his chariot toward Taraka, who saw the young god approaching and prepared to defend himself. The two fought furiously, and as they did, soldiers

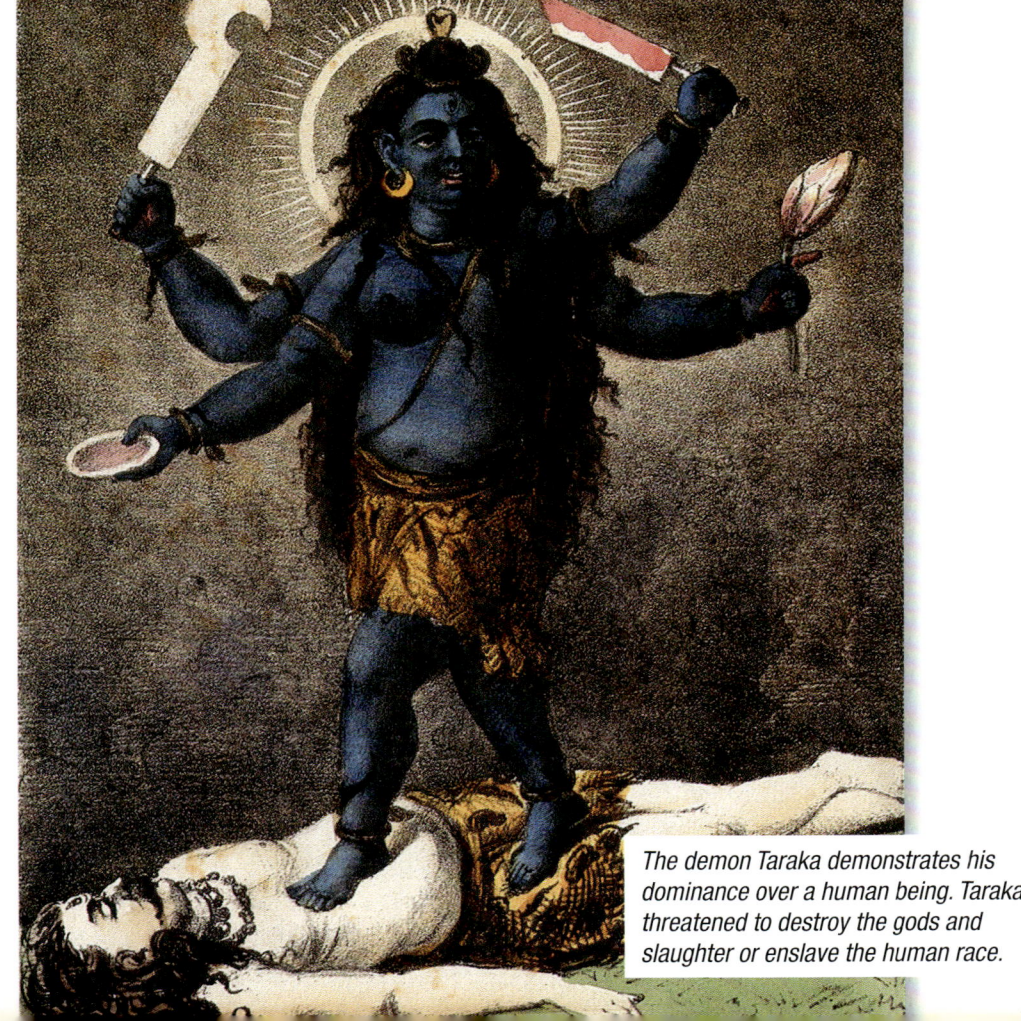

The demon Taraka demonstrates his dominance over a human being. Taraka threatened to destroy the gods and slaughter or enslave the human race.

from both sides gathered around to witness their leaders come to death grips. For several minutes the two traded blows with their swords, until the demon appeared to tire. A flash of fear transformed his face, and suddenly he turned to flee. At that, his opponent grasped his javelin and hurled it with his full might. The weapon passed straight through Taraka's body. The demon teetered back and forth for a second and then collapsed into the blood-soaked earth. Seeing their leader fall, the rest of the demons turned and ran, bringing the short but bloody war to a close.

Real and Legendary Warrior Classes

The war between Taraka's demon army and the gods and humans led by the war god Kartikeya is only one of dozens of wars of various sizes described in ancient Indian mythology. In fact, war and warriors are among the most prevalent themes in the entire corpus of Hindu myths. That reality reflects the fact that ancient India was never a united nation, as it is today. Instead, it was an enormous patchwork of rival kingdoms that rose, fell, and sometimes absorbed one another over the course of many centuries. Wars among the Hindu nation-states were therefore common, and this was bound to be reflected in their myths.

As a result of the prevalence of periodic warfare, each Indian kingdom maintained a warrior caste, or class—collectively called the Kshatriyas. The latter's importance in society was seen as second only to that of the highest caste, made up of the priests. Not surprisingly, the most successful warriors were highly revered.

Yet those real human fighters were far from the equals of the legendary warriors of the Hindu myths. This is because in those stories even the human heroes usually had some sort of special superhuman traits, including various magical abilities. A typical example was Ghatotkacha, son of the hero Bhima, who slew the demon Baka.

Kshatriyas
The caste, or social class, made up of warriors in ancient India

Ghatotkacha wages war with the help of human soldiers and animal-headed demons. His special magical abilities gave him many advantages on the battlefield.

Although Bhima was human, he married a demoness named Hidimbi; therefore, Ghatotkacha was half demon. That gave him the abilities to fly and to grow larger or smaller at will, which were clearly significant advantages in battle. In the breakdown of warrior classes within the Hindu myths, he was one of the Atirathis. Each Atirathi supposedly possessed the strength and skill to defeat ten thousand ordinary soldiers simultaneously. (Some sources put that number at sixty thousand.)

Atirathis
Mythical ancient Hindu warriors, each of whom was capable of defeating ten thousand ordinary soldiers

Following Strict Rules of Warfare

Some of the wars of Hindu mythology were fought strictly between human groups. For instance, the ancient Indian holy books

From Ancient India to a Galaxy Far, Far Away

The theme of warfare that pervades ancient Indian mythology has had an enormous impact on modern culture, not only in India itself but on a global scale as well. In large part this was the result of the worldwide popularity of producer-director George Lucas's colossally successful series of *Star Wars* films. Those films also inspired large numbers of equally popular animated movies, novels, comic books, video games, action figures, and children's toys. Lucas's first three *Star Wars* epics—*A New Hope* (1977), *The Empire Strikes Back* (1980), and *Return of the Jedi* (1983)—were heavily influenced by the *Ramayana*. From that great Hindu literary work, Lucas took the concept of a heroic young man who allies himself with a princess and battles an evil, demon-like villain. Instead of setting the story in ancient times, however, Lucas placed it in outer space, in a "galaxy far, far away." Another major element in the films that came from the Hindu myths is the concept of a powerful universal spirit that inhabits all life. Hinduism calls it the ishvara; in the *Star Wars* universe it is called "the force."

known as the Vedas mention the War of the Ten Kings, fought between rival clans from opposing powerful families. Similarly, the grandiose *Mahabharata*, supposedly recounting events of the ninth century CE, is largely built around the legendary Kurukshetra War. The story is set in the influential kingdom of Kuru, situated in north-central India. And the combatants are the Kauravas and Pandavas, rival clans of that region's most powerful family.

 The *Mahabharata* first presents a series of related myths that establish the background of the war and the many key characters on both sides of the conflict. Then the work portrays the climactic battle—involving almost 4 million soldiers. One of the most fascinating aspects of this and some other mythical ancient Indian wars is that representatives of the two sides meet before the great battle and agree to abide by strict rules. First, the fighting must start exactly at sunrise of a given day. Also, on each successive day of combat, both sides must quit the battlefield at sunset and not return until the following sunrise. In addition, it is expected that fairness and chivalry will be maintained at all times during the fighting. For example, multiple warriors are forbidden from attacking a single fighter, no soldier is allowed to kill an unarmed opponent, and no fighter from either side can attack a woman.

Bent on Seeking Revenge

Rules or no rules, however, the slaughter in that legendary battle was horrific. It was said that only twelve of the nearly 4 million soldiers survived, mostly members of the victorious Pandava clan. Thanks to the continued, wide popularity of ancient myths in India, that war and its climactic battle are known to every modern Indian schoolchild.

Yet even more famous and beloved in India is the chief mythical war fought not between human armies but rather between the demons and the gods, aided by their human allies. The leading characters of that iconic conflict—constituting the central event of the *Ramayana*—are Vishnu's heroic avatar Rama and Ravana, the evil, slimy ruler of the demon kingdom of Lanka. Ravana and his demonic generals professed several reasons for wanting to attack the gods and their human allies. But highest on the list was the desire to achieve revenge on Rama himself. For generations he had been the most prodigious slayer of demons in the known world. And Ravana had simply had enough. One day his demonic sister burst into Lanka's royal throne room, and according to modern myth teller Shahrukh Husain's retelling of the *Ramayana*, she approached the king and shouted, "Our brother Khar and all of his demons have been destroyed by Rama [and] he must be punished!"[19]

> **Lanka**
> The demonic kingdom ruled by the demon king Ravana

Ravana agreed, hopped onto his flying chariot, and hurried to the region where a powerful demon named Marich dwelled. "You must help me destroy this Rama and obtain his wife Sita for me," Ravana demanded of Marich. "Rama has killed 14,000 demons!" At first, however, Marich was fearful of going to war against the gods. "You do not know Rama," he told Ravana. "He is perfection personified and commands all the forces of goodness. You cannot defeat him."[20]

Furious at Marich's remarks, Ravana bared his teeth and said in a menacing voice, "How dare you contradict me? It is your place to obey. Now do as I say or I will kill you."[21] More frightened of Ravana than of Rama, Marich bowed low to his king and proceeded to help him raise a small army of bloodthirsty demons. Then Ravana put a demon general in charge of the horde and ordered him to destroy Rama and everyone associated with him.

Rama's Heaven-Forged Weapons

When the valiant Rama received word of the demon army's approach, he put on his armor, which was wrought of pure gold, and stood on a low hill located directly in his enemies' path. At the demon general's command, hundreds of Ravana's archers shot arrows at that lone figure on the hill. A passage in the *Ramayana* tells how Rama easily deflected those missiles. He did so with a shield that had been forged in heaven and thus could not be penetrated. Then he returned fire with his own bow, which also had divine properties. With that wondrous weapon, he swiftly let loose hundreds of arrows that "flew like serpents through the air, each seeking out its foe and piercing its heart. The demons shrieked and fell, like dry wood consumed by fire. Again and again Rama bent his bow like a sickle, sending forth the deadly arrows that seemed to darken the sun."[22]

Among the numerous demons that fell dead, pierced by Rama's divinely directed darts, was their general. The terrified survivors retreated to Lanka and reported what had happened to their king. Beside himself with rage, Ravana quickly raised a much larger army and took charge of it himself. Day and night he drilled his soldiers, preparing them for the coming war, in which he hoped to eradicate as many gods and humans as possible.

Although Ravana was evil and incredibly hideous to look at, he did possess at least some talent as a military commander. As a result, he correctly reasoned that when attacking a god it might not be enough to have thousands of fighters. It would be easier to kill Rama, the demon king reasoned, if he was somehow distracted and not thinking clearly. To that end, Ravana kidnapped Rama's human wife, Sita, and took her to Lanka under heavy guard.

When Rama found out what had happened, he was livid. He was determined to retrieve his wife, whom he loved dearly. He immediately informed his half brother and general assistant, Lakshmana, and the two rapidly raised the army they knew would be necessary to invade the demon kingdom. Among the fighters were several thousand monkeys, commanded by their general, the monkey-headed god Hanuman. As the offspring of Vayu, deity

In an effort to retrieve his kidnapped wife, Rama raised an army of monkeys commanded by the monkey-headed god Hanuman. Rama and Hanuman were ultimately victorious.

of the winds, Hanuman had the ability to fly. Hence, Rama ordered Hanuman to soar at top speed to Lanka, sneak into Ravana's palace, and tell Sita that her rescue was imminent.

The Strongest Force in the World

When Rama's army reached the demons' homeland, he wasted no time and ordered his soldiers to attack the capital city, also called Lanka. Expecting this assault, Ravana had amassed tens of thousands of demon fighters, and he was confident that he would finally achieve victory over his archenemy, Rama. As the opposing forces engaged in bloody combat, Ravana's son Indrajit rushed back and forth, hoping to find and slay Rama and Lakshmana. He did find them but succeeded only in wounding them. And that turned out to be of little consequence because Hanuman instantly healed them using a magical herb.

The conflict continued for more than half a day until most of the demon soldiers were either dead or had fled for their lives. Realizing his followers had lost, Ravana bellowed with rage and called his few surviving fighters mean-spirited names. Then he boldly stood in the center of the battlefield and challenged Rama to step forward and, if he dared, participate in single combat. Without a moment's hesitation, Rama rushed straight at the demon. In the next several minutes, according to the *Ramayana*, the two "tried to kill each other. Both were skilled archers, both knew all the science of warfare, both had weapons made by the high gods, and neither had ever known defeat. Each sent forth a cloud of arrows as they circled about each other, each had impenetrable armor and stood unwounded."[23]

Yet in the end Ravana had no credible chance. Marich's earlier prediction that the demon king would surely be defeated by Rama came true with a vengeance. Ravana eventually grew increasingly tired and less able to withstand the relentless attacks by Vishnu's powerful and heroic avatar. In the climactic moment, the huge demon fell from his chariot, and Rama seized that opportunity by

Agni Creates the New War God?

The Hindu god of war, Kartikeya, who defeated the demon Taraka in a well-known mythical conflict, was not the first war deity whom the ancient Indians recognized. During the Vedic period, in which Hinduism was in its formative stages, most Indians worshipped the god Indra as the overseer of warfare. Over time, however, Indra grew less popular in various parts of India and was replaced in that capacity by Kartikeya.

Multiple traditions developed to explain how Kartikeya rose to such prominence. Perhaps the most popular claims it was the very danger that Taraka posed to the gods and humans that motivated the creation of the new war god. Supposedly, Agni, god of fire, offered to fashion the new deity to ensure that Taraka would in fact be defeated. In that tale, Agni hurried to a distant monastery and mated with the wives of six wise men who dwelled there. All six women became pregnant. The question of which of their newborns to choose as the new deity was solved when a group of gods placed the babies in an enchanted garden. There, the six infants fused into one—who swiftly grew into the new war god, Kartikeya.

---

forcefully slicing off his opponent's hideous head. After that, most of the surviving demons fled, and over the years that followed, the demon kingdom steadily declined and disappeared from history.

Meanwhile, Rama was reunited with his wife, the lovely and gracious Sita. Despite the dangers each had recently experienced, neither had given up hope that they would ultimately prevail. After all, as was later written in the *Ramayana*, Rama did represent the strongest force in the world—goodness. Therefore, as was befitting, after having been "reunited with his beloved," the greatest hero of them all "experienced the happiness he deserved."[24]

CHAPTER FOUR

Karma and Destiny

It was snowing at the base of Mount Kailash, the sacred peak that rose in the highlands of northeastern India. The majestic god Vishnu, often called the world's protector, rode through the storm atop his trusty eagle, Garuda. Upward they went until they reached the impressive palace of the mountain's chief resident—the deity Shiva. It was Shiva's job to wipe away old, outmoded aspects of life to make way for new ones.

Desiring to speak to Shiva alone, Vishnu told Garuda to wait outside the palace's front gate. And for a while the obedient eagle sat quietly, enjoying the view of several nearby mountains. Abruptly, Garuda caught sight of a small bird sitting on a rock nearby. As he marveled at the little creature, the quiet scene was interrupted by the appearance of Yama, god of death. Perched on the back of a buffalo, Yama looked at the little bird on the rock, then dismounted and sauntered through the front gate, apparently intending to visit Shiva.

It disturbed Garuda that Yama had glanced at the little bird. "In ancient Hindu thought," Indian astrologer and myth teller Sandra Trishula Das points out, "even a slight glance of Yama is said to be the harbinger of death. Garuda, who had observed Yama's action, told himself, 'Yama looking intently at the bird can mean only one thing—the bird's time is up. Perhaps on his way back he will carry away the bird's soul with him.' Garuda's heart was filled with pity for the helpless creature."[25]

Garuda felt so bad for the little bird, in fact, that he decided to try to save it from the death deity. To that end, the eagle swiftly scooped up the tiny feathered creature and at top speed carried it to a forest thousands of miles to the north. The eagle managed to make it back to Shiva's palace gate just as Yama was leaving. Mustering the nerve to address the imposing god, Garuda asked why he had earlier glanced at the little bird. Yama answered that he had done so because he had suddenly received a vision of the bird being eaten by a serpent in a forest situated far to the north. Yama said he was puzzled about "how this tiny creature would traverse the thousands of miles separating it from its destiny in such a short time."[26]

At that moment, Garuda realized a mind-bending truth. Namely, it had been the bird's destiny to die in that northern forest. And Vishnu's loyal eagle had been an unsuspecting accomplice to the mysterious hand of fate.

The exquisite palace of the powerful god Shiva stands on Mount Kailash (pictured), a sacred peak in the highlands of northeastern India.

The Principle of Action and Reaction

Another way of seeing what had happened, Garuda concluded, was to attribute it to the law of karma. That aspect of fate, he knew, was an exercise in the mechanics of cause and effect, or put another way, the law of action and reaction. That is, an individual's actions can and do influence his or her future, or fate, or destiny. Moreover, if those actions are positive and consist largely of good deeds, the result is good karma, or a positive future outcome. Conversely, if the person's actions are negative—that is, consist of bad deeds—his or her future will be negative or unhappy in some way.

> **law of karma**
> The concept that good or bad actions can have consequences later in life or in the next life

The basic principle behind karma is not peculiar to ancient India. Indeed, great thinkers ranging from Jesus to the noted Greek scholar Aristotle to the brilliant Eng-

Vishnu's loyal eagle, Garuda, realized a mind-bending truth about his fate. That realization led to his discovery of the basic principle of karma.

lish scientist Isaac Newton have espoused some version of that concept. For instance, when, according to the New Testament, Jesus was arrested by agents of Jerusalem's high priests, one of those agents drew his sword. Jesus advised him to lower the weapon because "all who take up the sword will perish by the sword."[27]

> **transmigration of the soul**
> Reincarnation, or the idea that after death the soul is reborn in a new physical form

What makes the Indian version of karma different and almost unique is that both Hindu mythology and Hindu religion tie it to a belief in the transmigration of the soul. More commonly called reincarnation, it is the notion that after a life form dies, it is reborn in a new form. Furthermore, that continues to occur in generation after generation. In the words of noted meditation instructor Patrick Zeis:

> This means that while an individual who acts piously throughout their life will be born into more favorable circumstances in their next life cycle, an individual who acts unethically will be placed in a worse situation than the one they currently enjoy. Yet still, despite the fact that many assume this equates to a God-given fate, the Hindu scriptures tell us that since each of us has the power to think and act out of free will, we are in fact the masters of our own destinies.[28]

Kamsa's Tale: Evil Begets Evil

These ideas are among the main themes of one of the best known of all the Hindu myths involving karma and human destiny—the story of Kamsa. That unfortunate individual became ensnared in a sort of cosmic chain of karmic destinies as his evil deeds in one lifetime brought about still more bad behaviors in later lifetimes. Initially, he was a demon named Kalanemi who committed various crimes until Vishnu slew him.

Karma and the Land of the Dead

The ancient Hindu mythological version of the concept of karma still strongly resonates in Indian society. Many Hindus believe that the god of death, Yama, and his realm—the land of the dead, often also referred to as the underworld—can affect the workings of karma. Indian scholar Ritu Sharma explains, saying:

> [Yama] determines [people's] future circumstances . . . on the basis of their past deeds. Chitragupta, his accountant meticulously classifies [human] deeds as debt or equity and submits them to Yama . . . [who] is also known as the god of order because he is totally dispassionate in his judgment. The land of the dead is where our pitr (ancestors) reside awaiting their rebirth. According to Hindu understanding of life and death, rebirth can happen only when an offspring or descendent left behind in the land of the living produces a child.
>
> When a Hindu man or a woman dies, his/her children perform a ceremony known as "shraadh." During this ceremony, three generations of ancestors are invited to a meal and an offering of rice cakes is made. This is symbolic of the promise to produce children and repay the debt to the ancestors.

Ritu Sharma, "Karma Sutra: Understanding Shraadh, and the Land of the Dead," *Indian Express* (Pradesh, India), September 14, 2017. https://indianexpress.com.

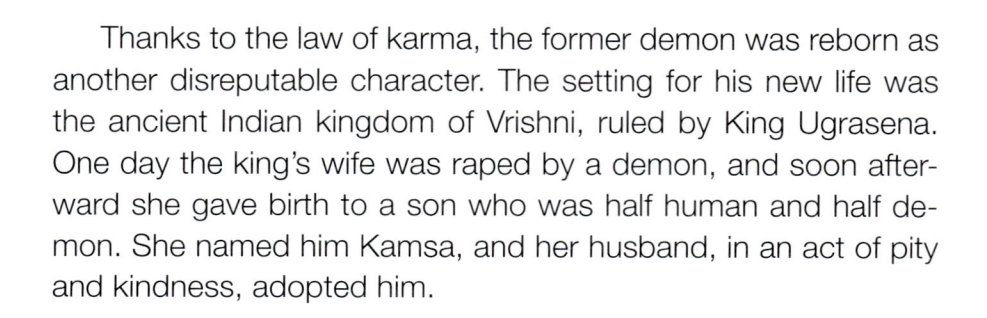

Thanks to the law of karma, the former demon was reborn as another disreputable character. The setting for his new life was the ancient Indian kingdom of Vrishni, ruled by King Ugrasena. One day the king's wife was raped by a demon, and soon afterward she gave birth to a son who was half human and half demon. She named him Kamsa, and her husband, in an act of pity and kindness, adopted him.

For years Kamsa hid his evil nature and pretended to be a virtuous, loyal royal prince. After reaching his early twenties, however, he showed his true self when he overthrew King Ugrasena. Not long after that, a soothsayer, or fortune-teller, told the new king that he was fated to be killed by the eighth child of his sister, Devaki. What could be done to keep that prophecy from coming true?, Kamsa wondered. He finally hit upon a plan in which he jailed Devaki and her husband and had each of their children murdered right after they were born.

> **soothsayer**
> A fortune-teller or mystic

Attempting to Evade His Fate

A number of years passed, during which Kamsa maintained his mean-spirited, bloody scheme designed to cheat fate and avoid the prophecy of his death. The king's advisers told him that Devaki's seventh pregnancy had ended in a miscarriage. Also, they said, her eighth pregnancy had produced a daughter, and per Kamsa's standing orders, that infant had been killed mere minutes after the birth. Because that eighth child was dead and Kamsa was still very much alive, he reasoned that he had successfully evaded his foretold fate.

But Kamsa was wrong. It turned out—as one of his advisers eventually revealed—Devaki had *not* miscarried her seventh baby. The princess had borne a son, whom she named Balarama. Moreover, her eighth child had also been a boy, not a girl. Thanks to the intervention of some unnamed god, the child had been reared in secret. Making matters even worse for Kamsa, the adviser stated, both Balarama and the eighth child—Krishna by name—had just arrived at the palace's front gate and sought an audience with the king.

Flustered and fearful, Kamsa quickly hatched a nefarious plan to do away with Devaki's two living sons, who appeared to be aiming to claim the throne for themselves. When Krishna and Balarama entered the throne room, therefore, Kamsa informed

Krishna straddles Kamsa's chest and beats him with his fist until Kamsa takes his last breath.

them that they had to prove themselves by fighting the city's finest wrestlers. Only if they defeated those athletes would the king grant them an official audience.

Of course, Kamsa expected the wrestlers to make short work of the two visitors. What he did not realize at that moment was that Krishna was not simply a human claimant of the throne but rather an avatar of the god Vishnu. The two brothers proceeded to quite easily defeat the wrestlers and then turned on Kamsa himself. The king was ready to flee, but Krishna grabbed hold of him before he could. According to a modern version of the Hindu text the *Bhagavata* (dating from around 800–1000 CE), Krishna

> immediately knocked the crown from the head of Kamsa and grabbed his long hair in his hand. He then dragged Kamsa from his seat to the wrestling [ring] and threw him down. Then Krishna at once straddled his chest and began to strike him over and over again. Simply from the strokes of his fist, Kamsa lost his vital force [died].[29]

The Good Along with the Bad

Thus it was that Kamsa's efforts to circumvent his true destiny came to nothing. In the end, the law of karma prevailed, just as it did for Vali, who was for a time the ruler of Kishkindha, a kingdom inhabited solely by monkeys. The monkey king was brave and the most skilled fighter in his country. Meanwhile, Vali's younger brother, Sugriva, acted as his second-in-command, and the two ruled in a just, fair manner.

Vali, however, had one weakness that, under the right circumstances, could potentially allow the law of karma to bring him low. That weakness was the tendency to lose his temper and jump to the wrong conclusion. Such a situation occurred during a

A God Intervenes

Here and there in the annals of Hindu mythology can be found indications that the law of karma is not necessarily absolute. Rather, those texts suggest that a god can intervene and change a person's karma. One Hindu myth that supports this idea is the story of Mrikandu. Mrikandu and his wife desperately desired a son, but the wife had long been unable to conceive. One day Shiva took pity on the couple, both of whom fervently worshipped that god. Shiva promised to give them a son, on one condition: the boy must die young. Mrikandu reasoned that a short life was better than none at all and accepted the offer. Sure enough, a few weeks later his wife became pregnant, and nine months after that the boy was born. They named him Markandeya. Gifted, he could talk when he was a year old and became a religious scholar by age ten. Sadly, however, when the boy reached sixteen, it became clear that he was dying. It was therefore a surprise to all involved when the death deity, Yama, failed to claim his soul. At the last moment Shiva unexpectedly stopped the process. Hugely impressed by Markandeya, Shiva had changed his mind and altered the boy's fate.

series of events beginning with the invasion of the kingdom by a large demon. Vali seized his club and boldly went out to fight the intruder, while the always-loyal Sugriva followed to back him up.

Seeing the monkey brothers approaching, the demon suddenly lost his nerve and ran away. Vali and Sugriva pursued the creature, which ran inside a dark cave. Vali told his brother to wait at the cave's mouth while he went inside to capture the monster, and Sugriva obeyed. Then suddenly, a cave-in blocked the entrance, trapping Vali inside. Sugriva and the other monkeys lacked the strength to move the huge stones blocking the way, so Sugriva dutifully waited, hoping some miracle might occur and free his brother. Months went by, however, and when Vali still did not appear, Sugriva felt he had no other choice but to rule the kingdom himself.

Eventually, thanks to some unanticipated earth tremors that dislodged some of the stones, Vali managed to escape the cave. Angry, he jumped to the mistaken conclusion that his brother had trapped him inside the cave. Vali unfairly cursed Sugriva and banished him from the country. Things looked bad for the exile until, unexpectedly, the hero Rama happened by. The latter did his best to mend relations between the two brothers, but Vali remained angry. Indeed, the monkey king was about to slay his brother when in desperation Rama fired an arrow to stop him.

As Vali lay dying, he finally realized that it had all been a tragic misunderstanding. "This life is full of sorrow," he told Rama (in a modern retelling of the myth by University of London scholar Stuart Blackburn). "We go on living, dying, born again to live and die, endlessly. Karma causes all this, and karma is caused by good and evil acts, and those acts are caused by . . . desires, which come from ignorance."[30] Driven by his own ignorance of the situation, Vali admitted, he must succumb to karma and pay the price. After he had taken his last breath, Rama, Sugriva, and all the monkeys grieved, while acknowledging that good individuals are subject to karmic law as much as bad ones.

CHAPTER FIVE

Fabled Animals

The fun-loving elephant-headed god of wisdom and learning, Ganesha, was (and remains) one of the most popular and beloved of all the Hindu deities. As Shahrukh Husain puts it, "He was known for his great loyalty to his parents and was often sent into the world to teach lessons in humility to mortals who were growing arrogant. But he is best-known for being the remover of obstacles and the bringer of good luck and is still worshiped before important undertakings."[31]

Indian artists have long depicted Ganesha not only as having an elephant's head but also as possessing only a single fully intact tusk, the other one having been partly severed at some point. Multiple ancient tales purport to explain how that situation came about. In one, Ganesha had a disagreement with Parasu-Rama, one of the many avatars of the god Vishnu. Things got physical, and during the tussle Parasu-Rama swung his ax in the elephant deity's direction. The weapon struck one of Ganesha's tusks, slicing half of it off.

In another and more often cited myth, Ganesha complained of an upset stomach after gorging on a large basket of candies, which were among his favorite treats. In an attempt to ward off the discomfort, he rode his vahana—a big mouse named Kroncha—into a small forest, hoping the wonders of nature would prove a distraction. All was well until suddenly a snake slithered by. The creature caught Kroncha by surprise, and he stopped short, causing Ganesha to topple over onto the ground. The force of the fall made the deity's pot belly break open, and out spurted several of the candies he had earlier eaten.

Very laid-back and not given to panic, Ganesha tranquilly retrieved the treats and popped them back into his belly. He wanted to make sure that they remained there, so he abruptly grabbed hold of the snake and wound it around his belly like a belt. When this happened, the elephant god heard a hearty laugh and glanced around to see where it had originated. It turned out

Ganesha, the elephant-headed god of wisdom, is widely known for removing obstacles and bringing good luck. Ganesha is one of the most popular and adored deities in Hindu mythology.

that the moon god, Chandra, had seen the incident and thought it was rather funny.

Though normally very good-natured, Ganesha did not enjoy being laughed at, so he decided to teach Chandra a lesson. Breaking off the lower half of one of his own tusks, the elephant-headed one threw it at the moon deity, who flinched and squealed and called Ganesha a nasty name. A week later the two made up and were friends once more. But ever since, in Husain's words, the elephant god "has been shown in his portraits with only one full tusk."[32]

Many Popular Animallike Deities

Ganesha and Kroncha were only two among many dozens of animal-shaped divinities populating the ancient Hindu universe. In mythological terms, they are termed theriomorphic, meaning "animallike" or "animal-shaped." Other notable vahanas of well-known gods include Nandi, the bull-like vehicle of Shiva, as well as the official gatekeeper of Shiva's stronghold atop Mount Kailash; the ram on which the fire god Agni rode; the peacock bearing the god of war, Kartikeya; the owl who carried Lakshmi, goddess of wealth and prosperity; and the donkey who served as vahana to Shitala, the goddess who was thought to fight disease.

theriomorphic
Relating to animal-shaped divine beings

Meanwhile, gods who were themselves theriomorphic—like Ganesha—were extremely popular in ancient India. Almost as cherished as Ganesha among those deities was Hanuman, the monkey deity who remained always the faithful companion to the hero Rama. Because Hanuman was the son of the god of winds, Vayu, the monkey god was sometimes referred to as Vayu Putra, or Son of the Air.

Another popular animal deity, Kamadhenu, sometimes called "the fervent one," was a cow-shaped being who represented the qualities of generosity and abundance. Over time, these traits helped shape the sacred image of the cow in Indian society. To

Indian society places high value on Brahman cows (pictured) because of their divine connection to the goddess Kamadhenu.

most Hindus, Indian historian Mukul Kesavan points out, the Brahman cow, which has a hump on its back, "is a beautiful thing." As for why, he says that in addition to the divine connection with the goddess Kamadhenu, the cow's "large eyes, its calm, its matte skin tinted in a muted palette that runs from off-white to grey through beige and brown, its painterly silhouette with its signature hump, make it the most evolved of animals."[33]

Still another highly popular animallike divine being in Hindu mythology is Narasimha, the so-called lion-man. He had the distinction of being the fourth avatar of the god Vishnu, and like some of that god's other earthly incarnations, Narasimha symbolized the divine wielding of immense power. His most celebrated deed was to destroy the horrible demon Hiranyakashipu. The latter had gained a special power that made him impossible to slay by either a man or a god. And that made him feel bold enough to declare war on all the gods at once. But Vishnu outwitted him.

By transforming into the lion-man, Narasimha, he became neither fully a man nor fully a god, but rather something unique, and that allowed him to subvert the demon's special power and kill him.

Vishnu's Serpent Companion

Another mythical animal that had a connection to the gods was Shesha. He was the large serpent whose coils enveloped and protected Vishnu when Vishnu and Brahma first encountered each other at the dawn of time. A member of a group of serpent beings known as Nagas, Shesha appears in a number of myths besides the one describing the world's creation by Brahma and Vishnu.

One of those stories deals with the great snake's origin and upbringing. According to the lengthy epic the *Mahabharata*, Shesha was born the eldest male offspring of a wise man named Kashyap and his wife, Kadru. The young serpent had numerous brothers, most of whom were cruel, violent, and destructive. Not wanting to be like them, Shesha left his parents' home and journeyed to some monasteries in the lofty Himalayan mountains lying north of India. There he spent many hours meditating and contemplating the meaning of life and nature of goodness.

Shesha also prayed often, and soon he caught the attention of the creator deity, Brahma. The latter appeared before the peace-loving serpent and offered to grant him a boon, or special benefit or privilege. Shesha asked only to be allowed to spend all his time observing the mysteries of life and the universe.

Lord Brahma disagreed with that objective. He said that a being as thoughtful and talented as Shesha should be doing more useful things, including helping the gods with various projects. The first task that deity assigned to the serpent was to travel deep beneath earth's surface, where huge boulders had recently been

> **Nagas**
> Intelligent serpents who appear in various Hindu myths

shifting and causing earthquakes. Following Brahma's instructions, Shesha, who was extremely strong, stabilized the great rocks and thereby made life on the surface quieter and safer.

Another task that Shesha took on was to become the frequent companion of the universe's chief protector, Vishnu. Often the huge serpent would accompany that god in his travels. And when the two approached a village or city, Shesha would enter the gates first and announce that the glorious divinity was about to appear. At other times, Shesha loomed behind Vishnu's throne or even bent his flexible body to form a seat for the deity. Moreover, even when Vishnu transformed into one of his avatars, the loyal serpent stayed at his side. When Vishnu visited earth as the hero Rama, for example, Shesha changed his own form to become Rama's brother, Lakshmana.

Mythical Animals in Modern Hindu Art

Modern paintings, sculptures, and other artistic renderings of Hindu deities often include the vahanas, or animals that provide transport, and often these creatures use their magical powers to assist the gods. Thus, paintings of Vishnu atop his trusty eagle, Garuda, abound in Indian art, as do images of Shiva riding a bull and the goddess Parvati riding a lion. The Hindu divinity perhaps most often depicted in modern artworks is the jolly Ganesha. According to spokespeople for New York's Metropolitan Museum of Art:

> With his elephant head and chubby, childlike body, Ganesha is the most beloved of all Hindu deities. He is the remover of all obstacles and so is called upon before the start of all kinds of ventures. . . . Sculptures of Ganesha are usually found at the beginning of a sequence of deities on the exterior walls of a Hindu temple, placed there to eliminate obstacles faced by the worshipper in his or her religious quest.

Metropolitan Museum of Art, *The Art of South and Southeast Asia: A Resource for Educators.* New York: Metropolitan Museum of Art, 2001, p. 31.

The Great and Powerful Bear King

Another mythical animal-shaped being who had a close connection with Vishnu was Jambavan, king of a race of Rikshas, or bears, who had a kingdom in the Himalayas. According to varying accounts in ancient Hindu texts, either Brahma created Jambavan to be Vishnu's helper or Vishnu fashioned the bear king himself, making the bear Vishnu's son. In whatever manner Jambavan arose, all the old accounts agree that he was incredibly strong—as powerful as 10 million lions. Also, it was said that the great bear was created in such a way that he could not be slain except by Vishnu himself.

One of the main myths involving Jambavan comes from the *Ramayana*, the story of Rama's war with Ravana, ruler of the demon kingdom of Lanka. At one point during a major battle, Jambavan encountered the demon king, and the two fought hand-to-hand (or more properly, paw-to-claw). Try as he may, Ravana was unable to kill his opponent, in part because Jambavan was so strong but also because the bear king was impervious to any death blows other than those of Vishnu. In contrast, Jambavan managed to wound Ravana in the chest, forcing him to temporarily retreat.

> **Rikshas**
> In Hindu mythology, intelligent bears who lived in a kingdom in the Himalayan mountains

Another well-known story about the bear king—one with a sad and tragic ending—involved a famous precious jewel called Syamantaka. Supposedly, any person who possessed it received eight cartloads of gold each and every day, making him or her increasingly wealthy. The gem was also said to protect its owner from evil. Satrajit, king of a northern Indian people called the Yadavas, was a loyal devotee of the sun god, Surya. That deity appreciated Satrajit's worship so much that he gave the ruler Syamantaka as a gift.

Eventually, Vishnu's avatar Krishna decided he must have the jewel for himself and demanded that Satrajit hand it over. The Yadava ruler refused, and when Syamantaka disappeared shortly

Jambavan, the king of a race of Rikshas in the Himalayas, was said to be so mighty that he could only be killed by Vishnu himself.

afterward, most people assumed that Krishna had stolen it. The reality, however, was that Satrajit had lost the gem in the forest where Jambavan lived in a cave, and the great bear had found it.

Meanwhile, Krishna wanted to clear his name by proving he was not a thief, and to that end he searched for Syamantaka. Eventually, he tracked the jewel to Jambavan's cave and asked the bear king to relinquish it. When Jambavan refused, a fight ensued, and the bear sustained a mortal wound. As Veronica Ions tells it, "Knowing he was about to die, Jambavan realized that his opponent could be none other than Vishnu, his father and beloved master in the previous age. At this, he begged forgiveness, gave Krishna the jewel, and offered him the hand of Jambavati, his daughter, who became one of Krishna's principal wives. Jambavan died glorifying the name of Vishnu."[34]

The Celebrated Giver of Knowledge

Long before he visited earth as Krishna, several ancient Hindu texts claim, Vishnu did so in the shape of a male human with a horse's head. The name of this avatar of Vishnu was Hayagriva, which combines the word for "horse"—*haya*—with the word for "neck"—*griva*. Hayagriva therefore translates roughly as "the one with the horselike neck."

In one of Hayagriva's traditional tales, back when Brahma and Vishnu were creating the world, Vishnu gifted Brahma with the four sacred texts called the Vedas. The original versions of those writings held potent powers that increased the strength of whoever possessed them. So two demons—Madhu and Kaitabha—stole them, hoping to become more powerful. They hid the Vedas at the bottom of the vast primeval ocean, and Brahma realized it would take him a long time to find them. So he asked Vishnu to help. For this mission, Vishnu assumed the form of the horse-headed Hayagriva, in part because his bushy mane was streaked with rays as bright as the sun. With them, he reasoned, he could more easily find the lost texts in the dark ocean depths. The horse-headed one proceeded to dive downward, found and killed the two demons, and retrieved the Vedas for Brahma.

Ganesha's Trip Around the World

The story of how Ganesha lost part of one of his tusks is only one of many myths involving that popular Hindu deity. Another tells how he and his brother, Kartikeya, god of war, argued over a piece of fruit, namely a mango. The two were strolling along a forest trail one day when they both caught sight of the mango at the same instant. Each wanted the tasty treat for himself, and they argued incessantly until the god Shiva happened by. In a friendly manner, Shiva suggested that the two try to settle the quarrel by holding a race around the world. Whichever deity won the contest, Shiva said, would get the mango. Ganesha and Kartikeya agreed to the plan, and the war god mounted his vahana, a peacock, and speedily flew away. Sitting atop his own vahana, a mouse, Ganesha appeared far less rushed. Smiling, the elephant-headed deity told the mouse to carry him around Shiva, which took about ten seconds. When Shiva seemed confused, Ganesha explained that to him, mighty Shiva was the whole world. And he had just traveled around it. With a wide grin, Shiva declared the clever Ganesha the winner of the contest and awarded him the mango.

Saving the sacred texts was an accomplishment that would echo down through the ages, because so much universal wisdom would otherwise have been lost and all of human history shrouded in the dark mists of ignorance. In the words of Kanakavalli Santhanam, an expert on ancient Indian culture, this story "of retrieval of the Vedas is the main source of inspiration for Hayagriva being revered as the bestower of knowledge."[35] And to this day, each year the people of India celebrate that animal-headed hero's momentous achievement.

SOURCE NOTES

Introduction: Universal, Epic Themes
1. George M. Williams, *Handbook of Hindu Mythology*. Santa Barbara, CA: ABC CLIO, 2003, p. 1.
2. Williams, *Handbook of Hindu Mythology*, p. 3.
3. Roy Amore and Larry Shinn, *Lustful Maidens and Ascetic Kings*. New York: Oxford University Press, 1981, p. 5.
4. Madhur Jaffrey, *Seasons of Splendor: Tales, Myths, and Legends of Ancient India*. New York: Atheneum, 1985, p. 7.
5. Jaffrey, *Seasons of Splendor*, p. 124.

Chapter One: The Creation of the Universe
6. Quoted in Wendy Doniger, ed., *Hindu Myths: A Sourcebook Translated from the Sanskrit*. New York: Penguin, 1973, p. 187.
7. Quoted in Doniger, *Hindu Myths*, p. 45.
8. Quoted in Doniger, *Hindu Myths*, p. 46.
9. Quoted in Doniger, *Hindu Myths*, p. 180.
10. Quoted in Doniger, *Hindu Myths*, p. 183.
11. Quoted in Kant Singh, trans., "Nasadiya Sukta," Academia, 2022. www.academia.edu.

Chapter Two: Good Versus Evil
12. Sadhguru, "Krishna Stories: Exploring Krishna's Path of the Playful," Official Website of Sadhguru, 2016. https://isha.sadhguru.org.
13. Veronica Ions, *Indian Mythology*. New York: Bedrick, 1984, p. 114.
14. Ions, *Indian Mythology*, p. 115.
15. Quoted in Kisari M. Ganguli, trans., "Story of the Killing of Vritra," MahabharataOnline. www.mahabharataonline.com.
16. Deepa Agarwal, "Short Story: The Birth of Durga and Battle with Mahishasur," *Indian Express* (Pradesh, India), October 12, 2018. https://indianexpress.com.
17. Laura Amazzone, "Goddess Durga: A Divine Female Role Model for Our Times?," HuffPost, May 25, 2011. www.huffpost.com.

Chapter Three: War and Warriors
18. Kalidasa, "The Birth of the War-God," trans. Arthur W. Ryder, Internet Sacred Text Archive. www.sacred-texts.com.

19. Quoted in Shahrukh Husain, *Demons, Gods, and Holy Men from Indian Myths and Legends*. New York: Bedrick, 1987, p. 71.
20. Quoted in Husain, *Demons, Gods, and Holy Men from Indian Myths and Legends*, p. 71.
21. Quoted in Husain, *Demons, Gods, and Holy Men from Indian Myths and Legends*, p. 71.
22. *Ramayana*, trans. Hari P. Shastri, ed. Elizabeth Seeger. New York: Scott, 1969, p. 106.
23. *Ramayana*, pp. 212–13.
24. Quoted in Doniger, *Hindu Myths*, p. 204.

Chapter Four: Karma and Destiny

25. Sandra Trishula Das, "One of My Favorite Stories on Karma," *Goddess Vidya* (blog), October 13, 2012. https://vedicgoddess.weebly.com.
26. Das, "One of My Favorite Stories on Karma."
27. Matthew 26:52 (Revised Standard Edition).
28. Patrick Zeis, "Hinduism's Eternal Wisdom: Karma and Dharma," Balanced Achievement, September 25, 2017. www.balancedachievement.com.
29. Quoted in A.C. Bhaktivedanta Swami Prahupada, "The Killing of Kamsa," Krsna, the Supreme Personality of Godhead. https://krsnabook.com.
30. Quoted in Stuart Blackburn, *Inside the Drama-House: Rama Stories and Shadow Puppets in South India*. Berkeley: University of California Press, 1996, p. 86.

Chapter Five: Fabled Animals

31. Husain, *Demons, Gods, and Holy Men from Indian Myths and Legends*, p. 56.
32. Husain, *Demons, Gods, and Holy Men from Indian Myths and Legends*, p. 56.
33. Quoted in Soutik Biswas, "Why the Humble Cow Is India's Most Polarising Animal," BBC, October 15, 2015. www.bbc.com.
34. Ions, *Indian Mythology*, p. 108.
35. Kanakavalli Santhanam, "Hayagriva—the Bestower of Knowledge," Fundamatics, January 9, 2020. https://fundamatics.net.

KEY HINDU GODS

Brahman

Brahma + Saraswati

Vishnu

Vishnu + Lakshmi

Rama* + Sita   Kalki*   Krishna*

Hanuman
(Rama's Loyal Servant)

Parvati + Shiva

Manu + Shatarupa
(First Man) (First Woman)

Ganesha

Human Race

*Vishnu's avatars

FOR FURTHER RESEARCH

Books

Swami Achuthananda, *Rama and the Early Avatars of Vishnu*. Queensland, Australia: Relianz, 2019.

Editors of Dorling Kindersley, *The Illustrated Ramayana*. London: Dorling Kindersley, 2022.

Crystal Moon, *Hinduism: A Simple Guide to the Hindu Religion*. Charleston, SC: Amazon Digital Services, 2019.

Vatsala Sperling, *Classic Tales from India*. Rochester, VT: Bear Club, 2020.

Internet Sources

Art of Living, "The Symbolism of Ganesha," 2019. www.artofliving.org.

Subhamoy Das, "10 of the Most Important Hindu Gods," ThoughtCo, June 25, 2019. www.thoughtco.com.

East Asian Cultures, "12 Most Prominent Hindu Demons," January 19, 2021. https://east-asian-cultures.com.

Kisari M. Ganguli, trans., "The Story of the Killing of Vritra," MahabharataOnline. www.mahabharataonline.com.

Hinduwebsite.com, "Brahman: The Supreme Self," 2019. www.hinduwebsite.com/brahmanmain.asp.

Neha Patel, "Hindu Epics: Are They Myths?," Book Riot, September 8, 2021. https://bookriot.com.

Donna Rosenberg, "The Creation, Death, and Rebirth of the Universe (Hindu Creation Myth)," Genius, 2022. https://genius.com.

Surrealist.org, "Story Matters." https://surrealist.org.

Websites

Hinduism, History.com
www.history.com/topics/religion/hinduism
One of the best overall websites on the internet about Hinduism, this offers the basic facts behind Hindu gods, beliefs, sacred writings, rituals, and much more.

Indian Mythological Stories, KidsGen
www.kidsgen.com/fables_and_fairytales/indian_mythology_stories
This useful site contains links to dozens of individual ancient Indian myths, along with colorful pictures of various characters from those stories.

Mahabharata, Hindupedia
www.hindupedia.com/en/Mahabharata
Highly informative, this site provides dozens of links leading to a wealth of detailed information about one of ancient India's two great mythological epics.

INDEX

Note: Boldface page numbers indicate illustrations.

Abhimanyu (hero), 22–23
Agarwal, Deepa, 26
Agni (god of fire), 12, 37, 49
Amazzone, Laura, 27, 50
Amore, Roy, 7
animals
   as avatars, 12
   mythical, in modern Hindu art, 52
   popular deities as, 49–51
Aristotle, 40
Arjuna (hero), 22–23
Atirathis, definition of, 31
avatar(s), 12
   of Brahma, 8–9, **9**
   definition of, 12
   role in creation, 17
   of Vishnu, 44, 47, 50, 54

Baka (demon), 22, 30
Balarama (human), 43–44
Battle in the Clouds, 23–24
Bhagavata (Hindu text), 44
Bhima (hero), 22, 30–31
Bhoots (ghosts), 22
Blackburn, Stuart, 46
Brahma (supreme deity), 8–11
   avatar of, **9**
   creates first humans, 14, 16–17
   Vishnu and, 10, 11

Brahman (universal spirit), 8–9, 12
   Hindu view of, 17
   role of, 13
Brahman cows, 49–50, **50**

Chandra (moon god), 49
corporeal, definition of, 8
creation/creation myths
   Brahman and, 8–9, 13, 17
   cycles of, 13–14
   of four worlds, 9–12
   of humans, 14–17

Daksha (deity), 12–13
dance, 16
Darbas (demons), 21
Das, Sandra Trishula, 38
demons, 20–21, 28
Devaki, 43
Devi (god of light), 12
divine intervention, definition of, 5
Durga (goddess of justice/compassion), **25**, 25–27
Dyaus (sky god), 23

Gandharvas (celestial beings), 13
Ganesha (god of wisdom), 12, 47–49, **48**, 55
Garuda (eagle), **10**, 11, 38–39, **40**, 52
Ghatotkacha (hero), 30, **31**

Gowariker, Ashutosh, 26
Grahas (demons), 21

Hanuman (monkey-headed god), 12, **35**, 35–36, 49
Hayagriva, 54–56
Hayagriva (avatar of Vishnu), 54
Hinduism
    key gods of, **59**
    as monotheistic religion, 13
    mythical animals in modern art of, 52
    view on Brahma, 17
Hinduism, History.com, 60
Husain, Shahrukh, 33, 47

India, map of, **6**
Indian Mythological Stories, KidsGen (website), 61
Indian mythology
    good versus evil as theme in, 22
    as a living mythology, 7
    universal themes in, 5–6
Indra (war deity/chief god), 23–24, 26, 37
ishvara (universal spirit), 13, 32

Jaffrey, Madhur, 7
Jambavan (bear king), 53–54, **54**
Jesus, 40, 41

Kadru (human), 51
Kailash, Mount (India), 38, **39**, 49
Kaitabha (demon), 55
Kalanemi (demon), 41
Kalidasa (Indian epic poet), 28–29
Kamsa, 41–45, **44**
karma, law of, 40–41

definition of, 40
land of the dead and, 42
Kartikeya (war god), 28, 29–30, 37, 55
    avatar of, 49
Kashyap (human), 51
Kauravas (clan), 32
Kesavan, Mukul, 50
Keshi (horse demon), 23
Kishkindha (monkey kingdom), 45
Krishna (avatar of Vishnu), 18–20, 23, 43, **44**, 53–54
Kshatriyas, definition of, 30
Kuru (Indian kingdom), 32
Kurukshetra War, 32–33

Lagaan: Once Upon a Time in India (film), 26
Lakshmi (goddess of wealth/prosperity), 12
land of the dead/underworld, 11, 42
Lanka (demonic kingdom), 33
Lucas, George, 32

Madhu (demon), 55
Mahabharata (Indian epic), 22, 24, 32, 51
Mahabharata, Hindupedia (website), 61
Mahishasura (Buffalo Demon), **25**, 25–27
Manu (first man), 14–17
Marich (demon), 34
Metropolitan Museum of Art, 52

Nagas (serpent demons), 20, 51
Narasimha (lion-man), 50–51
Newton, Isaac, 41

Pandavas (clan), 32
Panis (demons), 21
Pishachas (demons), 20
Pretas (evil spirits), 22
Prithivi (earth goddess), 23

Radha (goddess of love), 12
Rakshasas (demons), 20–21, **21**
Rama (avatar), 23, 33–37
   weapons of, 34
Ramayana (Indian epic), 23, 33, 37
   influence on *Star Wars* films, 32
Ravana (ruler of demon kingdom), 33–37
reincarnation, 41
Rikshas (intelligent bears), 53

Satapatha Brahmana (ancient text), 14
Sharma, Ritu, 42
Shatarupa (first woman), 16–17
Shesha (mythical serpent), 51–52
Shinn, Larry, 7
Shiva (major deity), 38, 45, 55
   dances honoring, 16
shraadh (ceremony), 42
Star Wars films, 32
Sugriva (monkey warrior), 45, 46
Syamantaka (jewel), 53–54

Taraka (demon), 28–30, **29**
theriomorphic, definition of, 49
transmigration of the soul, definition of, 41

Ugrasena (ruler of ancient kingdom), 42, 43
underworld, 11, 42

vahana, 9
   definition of, 11
Valanciunas, Deimantas, 26
Vali (monkey king), 45
Vayu (god of wind), 12
Vayu Putra (Son of the Air), 49
   See also Hanuman
Vedas (sacred texts), 9, 31–32, 55–56
Vedic age (c.1500 BCE–500 CE), 23, 37
Venkataraman, Swami, 16
Vishnu (deity), **10**
   in creation story, 10–12, 14–16, **15**, 18, 38, 55
   avatars of, 44, 47, 50, 54
   in modern Hindu art, 52
   serpent companion of, 51–52
Vishnu Purana (sacred text), 11, 12, 14
Vrishni (Indian kingdom), 42
Vritra (demon), 23–24, 26

War of the Ten Kings, 32
warrior classes, 30–31
Williams, George M., 6, 7

Yama (god of death), 4–5, 38, 39
   karma and, 42
Yama Kumar, 4–5

Zeis, Patrick, 41